MW00364922

PRAISE FOR *AGAIN*

The tone of *Again* is bleak, brutally satiric. Its voice is richly musical, deeply archetypal. And the combination is riveting. This collection's poet-Scheherazade resides in a house with "boards nailed over every window / and door, no entrance, no way out." But language does indeed give us a way to get out, a way to transcend. In this stunning indictment of American culture, the poet brings considerable talents to bear on making us achingly aware of the ingrained injustice in our society. Jennifer Perrine summons poetry's powerful devices to tell us the brutal truth.

—Paulann Petersen, Oregon Poet Laureate Emerita

The collective voice seems particularly hard to grasp at a time when our communities, country, and world deal so heavily in the currencies of isolation and fracture. But in *Again*, Perrine uses that collective voice to offer us a poetic (and prophetic) antidote to the long tradition of American exceptionalism. While myth-making implies invention, particularly of the grandiose kind, myths also remind us of those core truths of love, fear, intolerance, and hope that we live our lives by. Perrine turns the bombastic on its head in these poems and gives us the myth of our country's current moment in a voice at once Greek chorus and intimate monologue, reminding us of the very shared humanity we cannot afford to ignore.

—Keetje Kuipers, author of *All Its Charms*

OTHER TITLES FROM AIRLIE PRESS

AGAIN

AGAIN

_____ Jennifer Perrine

Airlie Press PORTLAND OREGON
2020

Airlie Press is supported by book sales and grants, by contributions to the press from its supporters, and by the work donated by all the poet-editors of the press.

P.O. Box 68441
Portland OR 97268
www.airliepress.org

email: editors@airliepress.org

Cover and Book Design: Beth Ford, Glib Communications & Design

First Edition
ISBN: 978-1-950404-03-2
Library of Congress Control Number: 2019957030

Printed in the United States of America

JENNIFER PERRINE

CONTENTS

e pluribus

INCREDIBLE 29	31 BEAUTIFUL
HONESTLY 32	33 PRESS
NATION 34	35 FAIR
DOG 38	39 DISGRACE
BIG 40	41 DISGUSTING
WEAK 42	43 TRADE
REALLY 45	46 LEADER
SAD 47	49 DEAL
FANTASTIC 50	51 CROOKED
STRONG 52	54 AMAZING
BAD 55	56 NOBODY
BAN 57	58 AND

_____ *unum*

_____ *et al.* _____

63 MAKE

64 AMERICA

66 GREAT

67 AGAIN

E PLURIBUS

TREMENDOUS

We woke to find the creature hovering
over us. We gnawed our lips, eyed its hooves,
imagined trampling. We bowed down so it

might see fit not to smash us. When we grasped
we might yet survive, rough flowers blossomed
on our fingers. We garlanded the great

creature with homespun roses, wrapped its horns
with petals. Our arms grew tired, but we kept
our weary hands raised in praise. When we could

worship no more, we fell back to the floor,
hoping the creature would not tear our limbs
from us. Silence was our final reverence.

For years, we did not speak, until our tongues
and teeth forgot words. We were sure the beast
could sense our faintest trembling. We waited

for the brute to make its move. When we died,
the creature kept roaring, never once touched
our bones, never even knew we were gone.

_____ TERRIFIC

When the angels came
to our land, we could
not fathom our good
lot. We could not shield
ourselves against their
strangeness fast enough.

❀

When they washed ashore,
there was no whirlwind,
no cloud of amber
fire. There were thousands
of dread faces. There
were no survivors.

❀

We did not touch them.
We heard the breaking
surf fussing over
their wings. We could not
ignore their message,
could not send them home.

RUDE ✳✳✳

No unwrought
state before
he broke us

open, carved
our marble
into his

art, crafted
rough creatures,
ornaments

he called forth.
No model—
he believed

we were trapped
in the slab,
knocked off stone

with controlled
strokes to find
us hidden

in shattered
parts. No rasp
nor riffler

to refine—
he desired
featureless

beasts, liked us
dull, could not
stand our shine.

FIRST

And now, in this circle, the poets, philosophers, men of science and of state, those who wait in limbo, who chose virtue yet have no hope of exiting the abyss. How exquisite the meadows of hell, green and gated, fed by a brook. We know this is the entrance to the steep decline, to the halos of lust and gluttony and greed, and deeper into violence, into the center of treachery. Forget those rings, their punishments. Let's remain among the guiltless damned, end our journey before we reach the place where no thing gleams, the spectacle of hoarders and spendthrifts pelting each other with their great weights. Let's put behind us the sullen waters and thorny trees, the plain of burning sand. We need no more reminders that such ditches exist. Ignore the torments, faint cries of panderers and hypocrites. Pay no mind to the renowned beast trapped in ice at the core of our world. Neglect the whir of its wing-beats, its vain weeping. We have no time to descend to those spheres. We belong here, just this side of the river, among the most decent of sinners.

_____ WORLD

We are of but not in it. We leave prints
in mud, a blaze of crumbs to mark our path
through vacant tracts. Snow fills our hollow steps.

We withdraw into our flesh. We relax
into astonishment, watchers behind
glass. We cannot smell the tires burn, the plush

pink smoke that chuffs from stacks. For all we know,
the ocean still exists beyond the reach
of our sunrise, sunset. We won't venture

out until it's safe again. We're busy
with danger. We have known the best of both
patting our own and pressing weight on backs,

footfalls on shoulders. Our better angels
and devils crouch close, hunch over, whisper:
We're not long for this. We wouldn't miss it.

_____ WONDERFUL

A finger
of flame shoots
through darkness,
portends, begs
us to watch,
though we don't.
We wander

instead through
rooms of rare
beasts struck dead,
pinned to walls
or stoppered
in bottles.
While the sky

spits comets
and eclipse
throws shade on
the hunger
moon, we peer
through thick glass
at the jaws

of creatures
amassed in
rows, long bones
and twisted
tusks. We gawk
at treasures
formed in strange

wombs, enter
chambers where
we can't catch
sight of slabs
of night cracked
to expose
light falling

from a time
before our
small marvels,
our boxes
and baubles
that never
cease to please.

_____ EXPLODE

The whole audience
booed, hissed, wished us off
this stage. In the air,
layers of upflung

dust, fragments of us
floating through the crowd.
Their claps and stamping
grew thunder-loud, tide

that rose, carried us
in the wind, gathered
grit in clouds of smoke.
When, at last, the din

broke, we drifted: ash
settled upon each
scornful tongue, breath drawn
sharp into their lungs.

FRANKLY

no one gave
a damn. We
all sat calm.
Nothing shocked
us. We had
no limbs with
which to feel
numb. They rolled
in the screen.
We did not
wince at the
images.
We did not

close our eyes,
did not scream
or cry. We
watched the crowd
gather, heard
the chanting.
We could not
see the dead,
though we knew
they were there.
We twisted
our faces:
lifted brows,

slackened mouths.
In exchange
they fed us
more. We took
what they gave.
We endured.
We ignored
each other,
the bodies
beside us,
forgot how
many of
us there were.

POLL

We pose
no threats
to them
that bred
us, take
less space
without
our horns.
They've left
us just
cower
and cud,
slow prey.
These scurs
will wreck
no fence,
won't keep
the wolves
at bay.

———— WALL

We scaled its face
even in sleep,
picked at cracks, gaps
in the mortar.
Bricks disappeared
into our fists,
first magic trick

of this prison.
We hid our best
confidences
in crevices,
flinched as the great
gray wave encroached.
We knew it must

fall. Still, we crouched
beneath to block
the blasts of wind.
We tagged our names
across its span
so we might know
if we belonged

to a herd penned
or if we were
lords hemmed in stone
enclosures, safe
from prying eyes —
no gate, no way
to leave or stay.

_____ BUILD

They built a bower. We were not allowed to rest

in its shade. We built a tower that loomed over

their crops. Sun-starved, they built a machine, planted it

in our fields, painted it green so we would not see

it snatching our feasts from beneath our feet. We built

a god that hooked its jaws through their children. They built

a new universe. We watched them go, built gardens

in their ruins. We grew restless, built a rocket.

Inside, we travel across galaxies looking

for their land. We build each day new ways to make them

come home. We build up our hopes that this time they'll stay.

CARNAGE

We
did
not
want
to
fight,

so
we
turned
our
bones
out

of
our
skins.
We
made
them

march
in
rows,
sent
them
in

our
stead.
They
ran
through
streets

with
knives
held
high.
They
came

with
guns.
The
beasts
we
bore

tore
out
our
tongues.
We
could

not
stop
them.
They
were
good

at
their
work.
They
said,
we'll

take
care
of
you.
They
said,

be
still,
this
will
not
hurt.

DISASTER ✳✶✳

We survived underground: gray
water recycled, shelves piled
high with medicine and food.
Of course we had guns. Who knew

what creatures or intruders
might breach our doors? We waited
for the air to clear. The old
ones said we were safe down here.

They claimed they were our parents,
that we'd never been beyond
the bunker. They lied. We lived
outside. How else would we know

the give of earth underfoot,
the gloss of sun on our skin?
No matter. We took the guns.
We sent out the elders one

by one. None came back. We make
children now in this dark room,
whisper to them of the sea
and sky. One day we'll send them

out, too. For now, we keep watch
on the supplies, each other,
the guns. We sip shallow breaths.
We remain buried, alive.

PEOPLE

When we came to this land, we found
it empty save for these creatures.
They grunted like children or gods,
ineffable. We hunted them.
We kept them as pets, well-behaved.

We called reinforcements: women
to care for their cubs, men who prayed
and shot to stop their infernal
racket, the squawks when they'd escape
their pens. Some of us went mad, claimed

to make sense of their babble, tried
to take them as wives. Not once was
I tempted, not even when one
whispered in my own tongue. I knew
what must be done. Now, see: they're gone.

LOSERS

We played the hands we were dealt. We were not sore, unsportsmanlike. We conceded defeat from the start. The crowds threw ticker tape parades, filled fields with snow, asked us to lie down to make angels or corpses. We rolled the dice. We came up short. We roused for days

of marching through brambles and thorns. In the distance, we could hear their hunting horns. Stags and foxes, we left prints in mud, our scent for dogs. We drew short straws. Our lovers welcomed home dark horses who outstripped us, the doppelgangers who go where we cannot.

_____ LOVE

After, we do not know what to do
with our hands, how to gentle them, perch
them tame upon another's body.
When our loves whistle in the kitchen,

they mortar us. We seek shelter, press
our snouts to their fur but cannot find
their scent. We learn to touch with our eyes
first, not to look beyond at the sand

that tracks through the halls. In bed, we hear
the curtains flap like canvas. We rest
under cover of our armaments.
In our chests, the machine still pulses.

GOING

When our travels got tough, rocky
turf and snowdrift, we strained our necks
taut against the bridle. Our hips
and ribs rose from our skin, our coats
grew thin. Winter fell and we found
no pasture. We changed hands, prodded
round the auction ring. Lashed, we spun
in everlasting ruts. The pen,
at least, we shared. I did not mean
to kick and bite, but I thirsted,
the stall was so small. Forgive me.
When the men raise their numbers, fair
price for our ugly bones, think how
I placed my face to your withers.
When the bidding has closed, hear me
nicker and whinny. In our sleep,
we race the long distance beside
each other, ground easy under
our thunder, going, going, gone.

PATHETIC

We huddled, shrouded in the corners.
Our wounds were ample. We displayed them,
glistening red spectacles to prod,
to scorn. We were housed in the sorrow
cages, kept in pens meant to mimic

our native habitats. Children poked
sticks through the bars, fed us scraps, whispered
from behind the legs of their parents.
Some called for us to caper, to ape
their strange sounds. We did the best we could.

We ate their crumbs, smiled wide, shammed laughter
even when doubled over with hurt.
We refused them little. We waited
until they had turned their backs to weep.
We waited until they left to roar.

TOUGH

as nails driven
not to join but
to hook, as old
boots that still march
after poundings
they took on harsh
streets, as cheap cuts
of meat and jaw
muscles that flex

to tear and grind,
as tanned hide stretched
into a drum
and mallet swung
in steady time,
as thick tissue
formed over wounds,
as our armor
no ardor may

pass through, as spires
that rise like teeth
and drip with spit
in the dark caves
we fumble blind,
as the brittle
shell that signals
the ripeness of
the seed inside.

MESS

who served us who placed the dish stirred the pap that clung

to our lips who spilled the wine on the floor who called

out for more as we chewed the fat skipped from

one thought to the next slipped our tongues in the

mouths of friends we did not plan for how the meal

would end we jarred teeth loose on bread we gnashed and

gnawed we mashed fists on flesh to know touch we

could not help but give in to such fetes what lush digs

what land of rose and milk who doled out this fare each

course lapped from the bowl we shared who was it we once

dined with in this hall where we passed the plate licked clean

UNUM

_____ INCREDIBLE

I
am
cold
stone
you
wash
with
sun,
glint
with
your
long
tongue
of
light.
Warmed,
I
slip,
jut,

rip
free
your
mask,
god
who
hides
not
as
swan
or
bull
but
slick
gold
dredged
from
gray
beds.

What
makes
you
cling
to
the
edge
of
my
hard
arc,
calls
you
to
shine
on
my
rough
face,

rock
struck
with
flaws?
What
spurs
you
to
show
your
flare
and
fleck,
to
spend
your
glow
on
me?

_____ BEAUTIFUL

I wake up
in a snow
globe shaken
by your long
fingers. You
startle me
from my rest,
make me dance
upended,
make me fly
with no net.
It's not you
who catches
me but glass,
window through
which I watch

you watch me.
I am no
acrobat,
but I twist
to touch you.
When you leave,
I settle
my body
in drifts deep
enough to
swallow me.
In my sleep,
your hands still
hold my world,
you never
put me down.

HONESTLY

It wasn't quite right
to say I offered
myself to the king.
No sister waited
in his chamber, begged
for my tale. Alone,
I came by my will
to live the same way
as all the others,
only I knew lies.
He meant to take me

to bed or kill me,
I couldn't recall.
Either way, escape
hinged on how I made
fictions. A thousand
times I prayed for dawn
to break. It did not
matter I survived.
In the end, he named
me queen. His story
held more sway than mine.

no charges, though he deserves it. I cannot risk

the law, its long reach. There is no sanctuary,

only bigtooth leaves at their most golden, folded

between the pages of my prayer book. I preserved

what I could. I ironed his best shirt the morning

we married, let him plead his case again tonight.

We proceed, history heavy in our pockets.

My tongue runs over sockets where my teeth once were

white as the sun glinting on the river, shining

through blinds, falling on our bed, warming it with light.

_____ NATION

Go back where you came from, they said,
so I remain shut in this house,

boards nailed over every window
and door, no entrance, no way out.

_____ FAIR

I
spun
this
pink

sweet
to
scour
your

tongue.
I
swung
this

car
down
its
track

to
throw
you
back,

to
sick
you
up.

I
lowed
and
crowed

in
my
soiled
stall

so
you
might
pin

a
strip
of
blue

to
mark
me
first.

I
pursed
my
lips,

pressed
my
eyes
shut

so
when
you
sank

me
in
the
tank

I
would
not
gasp

nor
catch
your
laugh,

would
drown
in
this

wet,
sense
no
more

than
its
raw
grasp.

DOG

Do not let me off my leash. Keep me tethered, my gleaming teeth
forever in reach. Now you've tamed me, I'll cram my hackle, play
the wag. When you shut the door, I'll whine, left behind, but stow all
barks and howls, all bays that may offend. For you, I'll keep my snout
clean. For you, I'll end the prowl. You've put my wild to work, given
me this pristine bowl of water to lap, a groomer to smooth
my fur, to comb out the mats. Still, I can't help notice your scent

resembles the musk of the one who once called me mutt, kicked me
in the gut, sent me panting. Blood crusted where my ear was torn
by that cur. His voice—so much like yours—hounds my dreams, shouts *mongrel*
bitch, hunts until I bite, grip tight the bone, shake my head to break
the neck. I wake with snarl and slaver, strain against my silver
chain. Forgive my poor training, my bad deeds. He was my master,
but that is past. You're a different man. Yours is the hand that feeds.

DISGRACE

It's no shame when I fall to my knees in this hall of worship, when I shimmy up silk to slip from great heights, sleight of hand that shouts *here I am* and then makes me disappear. I stoop to conquer, get low to show I have not learned my lesson.

I strut, lift my skirts, reveal the sweat that slicks my shirt. I thrash my hair and stamp my heels against cement. The crowd says it's an embarrassment to dance this way— writhing with radiance in the face of collapse, all outthrust hips, punch-drunk fists—

even as they rise to cheer and clap. I make them sway in this ecstatic trance, help them to let go at last. They don't know and don't care what comes next. I undress my teeth, snarl for the audience: *You owe me nothing. I've bared myself for less.*

BIG

I've
made
my
self
a
sun,

sent
rays
through
space
to
touch

your
far
face.
Still
you
will

not
gaze
back.
When
I
blink

out,
may
the
cold
cut,
may

you
be
lost
in
the
dark.

DISGUSTING

This taste upon my tongue, I cannot douse it
with other flavors, cannot choose to savor
its bitter peel, its rough dregs. I cannot spit
away the sour twist, cannot rinse this out.
You put the words in my mouth. Now, their odor
lingers, shreds wedged between my teeth. I must chew
though my jaw is sore, though you've made nourishment
a chore. When I refuse, you refill my plate,
you intubate, disallow my hunger strike.

I cannot press my lips tight enough, cannot
rid myself of the reek. Please take your palate
to a connoisseur who will appreciate
what dishes you have on offer. I forsake
your daily bread. I will learn to feast again,
to believe sustenance can be sweet again,
clutch of grapes bursting their juice, honey dripped thick,
sluice of water. I will teach myself to crave,
hanker, remember food as more than fodder.

_____ WEAK

link most sure
to give when
hit, to split
to pieces,
I possessed
no unit
cohesion,
was not well
made, not forged
of the same
mettle as

my brethren.
I never
volunteered
to secure
this union.
Still, I played
my role. Now,
may this chain
collapse, may
no other
fill this hole.

_____ TRADE

I'll
ply
mine,

will
work
for

rhyme,
will
sing

for
food,
will

give
my
wrecked

blush,
my
love's

crushed
throat,
will

strip,
will
cut

you
a
deal,

peel
off
my

skin,
call
it

a
steal
when

you
crawl
in.

REALLY

I put my hands on your slick image, could not keep
up with the jump cuts. When I licked you, static seared

my tongue. I pulled the plug, watched you go cold. At last
I saw your true face in the flat black. Through the screen,

you glittered, ghost light. You could hold my gaze for hours
at a time, never blink. I synced my lips to yours.

LEADER

I thought if I threaded to the spool,
the dark room would fill with illusion
of movement, stills brought to life. It did,
but first I appeared: blank, nothingness.
I had prepared a song, but my voice
was reduced to a hum, a hiss heard
loud as a blare of horn: *make ready*.
They hushed for me. I was an angel
that way, no story of my own, just
this annunciation, countdown to
the feature, suspense before the show.

SAD

This day's bread
failed to rise.
I rapped it

with a thumb,
with a nail
tapped it. No

hollow knell,
no note when
my body

made contact.
What I thought
was alive,

thriving, is
only stone.
What I did

to kill it:
chemicals
in the tap

water, heat
shut off, no
leavening

in this room,
no daylight.
Still, it is

my only
sustenance,
this dense mass.

I swallow,
feel it sink
in my chest,

lodge its weight
in my gut.
I tear hunks,

mouth dry, jaw
aching, wait
for hunger

to subside
so I can
drop my knife,

push aside
these last crumbs,
say *enough*.

DEAL

My mother dealt in sorrows, passed them out in rounds, face down,

so we each received an even hand. She was every queen

in the deck. Her men dressed as the one-eyed jacks and the king

with the axe, blade behind the back or turned aside to stay

blind to her weeping. We each awaited our turn, unsure

whether to hold or to cut our loss. We all called, all checked.

She never claimed to know the rules, the difference between raise

and fold. She only knew the stakes. She placed us: her best bets.

FANTASTIC

Her wicked charms disarmed me.
She laced my bodice tight, combed
my thick curls and, poison-kissed,
put me to bed in a glass
casket. She made for me strange
prisons: woodland towers and homes

built of cake and confections.
Though I know she wished to keep
me secret, to devour me,
still I recall the woman
who climbed the moonless staircase
of my hair, the one who held

out a red apple, begged me
to take a bite. Now, I stand
before the mirror that speaks
the cold truth of the ever
after: each witch is no more
than the girl who once survived.

CROOKED

She crooked a finger at me and I was hooked, her little lamb sure
to go where her merriment went. I was out of joint, out in drag
as soft white meekness, garb to lure her in. I did not mean to fleece
or snow, though I admit it was criminal how I overlooked
the tender nooks where her veins showed, where I could have followed against

the rules, could have swindled the blue that shined through her skin, charmed her red
as her cloak. She left me with this smile that does not quite reach my eyes,
that cannot lie, that says *here I am*, though I make my best efforts
at disguise. Next time I will bare all my teeth, set strange in my mouth,
the better to greet, to taste, the better to break open in howls.

_____ STRONG

When
I
set
foot
in
that
plot,
I
thought
Eve
must
have
been
green

to
fall
for
that
slick
talk.
The
fruit
is
just
juice,
peel,
and
pit.

God
knows
how
to
tempt,
to
hold

out
flesh
we're
not
meant
to
taste.

I
won't
bite.
I
want
no
more
than
scent.
At
most,
I'll
lap
one

drop,
one
sip.
I'll
stop
short
of
the
full
grasp
of
good
and
sin.

AMAZING

In the myth I invent,
you do not hand your sword
to the man who will kill
me. You unspool your thread,
mark the route. We both know

the promise of a sure
way out. From the center,
the path back is a crease
pressed to your face by sleep.
I stop waiting for you

to retrace your steps, quit
plans to escape. You let
the wind scuttle your string.
Each night, I learn I can
devour and not be damned.

BAD

that I did not know the roots
of this word: *hermaphrodite,*
womanish man. Bad my flesh
cannot conform, can perform
to be mistaken for. Bad
when awakened with a kiss
am still embodied, when sleep
alone knows all my names. Bad
whenever Jill or Jack, notes
pricked backward, figure recoiled
in box. Bad as powerless
to shed dress, as had power
to suit but did not. Bad this
land I cannot touch, divide
too much. Bad about such terms,
such common ways of saying:
to identify what hurts,
I make of myself a slur.

NOBODY

I'm nobody. Who are you to tell me
I'm not, to craft for me a name that fits
slack as the bag in which I must carry
the clothes you chose to cover or expose
my nakedness? Who are you to assume
I wear flesh, inhabit space, can be kept
in this house of food and breath? Who are you
to say you can observe me plain as day,
sitting on your porch, sleeping in your bed,

standing in your kitchen, cooling my head
under the sink's tap? We are not a pair.
I do not make a sound, do not disturb
the air with movement or voice. I do not
fill my hollows with song, do not stretch stiff
limbs at dawn, do not make charms to ward off
the void. You think you're the true nobody.
You could be. The trick's not to disappear.
The trick is to learn you've never been here.

_____ BAN

I sever you with glass pipe, shotgun in our dealer's
car, spray paint in paper bag to force awe. I banish

your jaw working over some blue boy, dollar store gold
hoops swinging, slipped off before each fight. I cast out you

of leopard prints, of stolen bras and stilettos stuffed
to fit. I exorcise you who needed to be seen,

who drank and threw up on the kitchen floor, then returned
to drink some more. I exile you to a distant shore,

you who strung the night with stars, who swam in streams alive
with ice, who blew smoke, wafted it in clouds, tore tempests

through our hometown. Without you, the air is still. The path
I walk alone is clear and clean. May you remain gone.

May your shadow never haunt my door. I will not look
at the trail, tracks you left. I will not retrace your steps,

press against this thin partition, listen to you curse
and laugh, so close I could touch, I could welcome you back.

_____ AND

And after no one was left
to sing to sleep. And I dropped
the name of the one who took
both my wrists and spun me, forced
out and tethered to the ground.
And my thighs rubbed the backseat,
and my tongue in another
mouth was peace and stone my thumb
fluttered over. And I placed
my conscience in a cramped box

for authorities to keep
locked or spill open at will.
And when I added the sum
of my labors I found them
different in kind, strata
of sand and silt in a jar,
layers and lairs. And anthems
played long, and I raised my hand
to my heart, pounded my fist:
revive. Recover from this.

_____ ET AL.

MAKE

One is never born a woman.
All women are made, stitched from parts.
It takes practice to learn the art
of holding the pieces in place,
of coordinating the limbs
to glide and pivot as fashioned.
It takes ages to grasp what needs
you were built to suit, whose wishes
invented you, which hands labored
hours in secret chambers to form
you, kiss you awake. Every day,
you prepare before the mirror,
feign the face you will need to move
through this world as if you belonged
here, as if you weren't a mistake.

We
claim
you
as
our
own,
stone
we
heft,
cast
first
and
last,
no
sin,
no
shame
in
our
past.

We
tame
you,
plant
this
flag
that
grows
in
straight
rows,
keeps

watch,
blots
out
weeds
that
sneak
through
cracks.

We
name
you:
land
of
the
smack
that
makes
us
see
stars,
home
of
the
belt
that
stripes
our
backs.

GREAT ✗✦✦

Let crones
battle
over
east and
west. Let
girls fall

asleep,
poppy
fields lush
and red.
Let roads
appear

gold, let
strangers
link arms,
march off
toward our
greener

pastures.
We will
grant them
entrance,
help them
wake to

find it
wasn't
a dream,
it was
no place,
like home.

AGAIN ✶✶✶

We shift our
tongues to fit
words the world
compels us
to swallow.
We turn grit
to pearls, spit
them up and
out, from the
top, once more
with feeling.

ACKNOWLEDGMENTS

Many thanks to the past and present editors of Airlie Press, for inviting me into the collective and giving this book an entrance into the world.

Much of this collection was written during a fellowship at Vermont Studio Center, and I'm grateful for the time, space, and community that VSC offered. Thank you to all of the February 2017 fellows, especially those of you who read or heard a handful of these poems and encouraged me to turn them into a book. Special thanks to my Maverick neighbor, Sarah Coates, who pointed me to new source material and made me aware of so many more words that were calling out for poems.

ABOUT THE PUBLISHER

Airlie Press is run by writers. A nonprofit publishing collective, the press is dedicated to producing beautiful and compelling books of poetry. Its mission is to offer a shared-work publishing alternative for writers working in the Pacific Northwest. Airlie Press is supported by book sales, grants, and donations. All funds return to the press for the creation of new books of poetry.

COLOPHON

The poems are set in Cochin, originally produced in 1912 by Georges Peignot for the Paris foundry G. Peignot et Fils and based on the copperplate engravings of 18th-Century French artist Charles-Nicolas Cochin. The titles are set in Florence from Stereotypes. Printed in Portland, Oregon, USA.